Letters From Italy:
Confessions, Adventures, and Advice

Susan Van Allen

www.susanvanallen.com

Website design: www.bygonedesign.com

Cover design: Rick Crane, www.rcds.co

Author photo: Veronica Puleo,
www.verofoto.com

Mille Grazie to Patricia Sullivan, my
reader/editor/sister extraordinaire,
Amy Guglielmo, my writing *amica*, and all my dear
friends and family here and in Italy who have been
by my side and made these adventures possible.

To my Husband, Jon,
With Love and Gratitude

And to The Most Wonderful New Arrival
Step-Granddaughter Florence
I Wish You a Life of Beautiful Adventures

It loved to happen--

Marcus Aurelius

CONTENTS

Preface

The year I was born my grandparents took a trip to Italy. The story my Nana always told me was this: "When Papa and I got to Venice there was a Cablegram at our hotel, telling us Baby Susan was born. I ran around the lobby, out to the Grand Canal, telling everybody!" My imagination pans out to a vision of Nana calling my name to the gondoliers, and me, thousands of miles away in a Newark, New Jersey bassinet.

A few years ago, a stack of Nana's letters from her trip fell into my hands. They're written on onion skin stationery, in cursive that would make her nun teachers proud. Whether she was writing about the opera at the Baths of Caracalla, the Duomo in Florence, or the view of the bay of Naples, her words were the same: *"It's like a dream..."*

I piled my haphazardly written travel journals next to Nana's letters. Clearly I didn't inherit her tidy, proper style. But her passion for Italy and mine are in synch. Over my decades of traveling, Italy has been *like a dream* to me too--with twists, turns, awkward, and awesome surprises.

So here's the baby who gondoliers heard about long ago, who grew to love Italy more and more with each visit, sharing confessions, adventures, and a bit of advice with you about some of my favorite destinations.

Whether you're reading this in an armchair, as you're dreaming of your next trip, or on an airplane, I wish you *Buon Viaggio!*

Susan Van Allen
Ca Pisani, Venice

Letter from Rome: That's Amore

"I know a shrink in New York who sends women who are suffering from low self-esteem to Italy for a month," Heather whispers, as we clink glasses at a wine bar near the Campo dei Fiori in Rome.

My *amica* Carol nods toward a handsome Italian *signor* at the other end of the room, who's been staring at us since we walked in the door: "Men like that are better than Zoloft," she says. *Il Signor's* stare washes over us, blending in with the deep rich taste of red wine, the sharp pecorino cheese, the warmth of the rustic wood tables.

I have to admit the stare feels darn good.

I flashback to 1976 when I was 18 and arrived in Rome for the first time, when the flirting game was more primitive, played in the *Me-Man-You-Woman-Hubba-Hubba* style.

My "American Girl In Italy" experience began as soon as I stepped off the train, just as it was captured in the famous Ruth Orkin photo. There, a young woman walks in Florence while 13 men—from a guy in a T-shirt on a vespa to a group of older gents in suits--give her variations of the leering eye. The American Girl steels herself, looking like a frightened doe. The photo was taken in 1951, but in that sweltering August of 1976, things in Italy hadn't changed that much.

"*Signorina, signorina,*" men hissed from every corner. They popped out of nowhere, grabbing their crotches, reaching out for pinches. I was fresh American meat in their jungle.

According to my Catholic upbringing this reaction was all "through my fault, through my fault, through my most grievous fault." I was supposed to be behaving and dressing with "Mary-like modesty" so my body would never be an occasion of sin to others.

Varieties of guilt flogged me. I felt guilty for wearing a halter top, but it was too hot for anything else. I felt guilty for lying to the men who stopped and asked if I was lost—of course I was, but I wasn't supposed to talk to strangers, right? I felt guilty because I'd read *The Sensuous Woman* and wasn't FRIGID the worst thing a woman could be? I felt guilty because Gloria Steinem had ordered me not to be objectified—should I be kicking these guys where it hurts?

At a loss, I assumed the *American Girl in Italy* walk, with my mother's mantra in my head: "Don't encourage them." This strategy became futile in The Forum when a man who'd been stalking me, hissing behind every pillar, finally lost control at The House of the Vestal Virgins, ran up and slung me over his shoulders in a fireman's carry, squeezing my behind like a ripe tomato. I beat on his back and hollered till he dropped me and ran off laughing.

Shaken to the soles of my Buffalo-sandaled feet, I brushed myself off. *Did that just happen to me? Me, the high school drama club geek? Me, the one who stood watching the girls with their flawless Farrah Fawcett hairdos get smooched up against their lockers by the cool guys?* I scurried for my guidebook and squelched the confusion by reading about how the Vestal

Virgins served Vesta, the Goddess of the Hearth, by keeping her flame continuously burning and maintaining a vow of chastity for 30 years.

But that moment of being airborne, pinched, and that laugh—particularly that laugh--kept playing back. As if it was a grown-up game of tag and I'd just had my initiation.

Thirty years later, Italian men have refined their flirting style to an art form I rank up there with the country's many masterpieces. I've watched it evolve over many years coming here. It's as if they were all sat down and ordered to view Marcello Mastroianni movies, memorizing his looks and moves to perfection. Now what's in their genes, in their historical legacy from the days of Casanova, has come to full flower. Women are adored here--from precious baby *principessas* to *mammas* and everything in between.

And who doesn't adore being adored? Having reached that certain age where attention back home is waning, here it comes at me with every encounter. The *barista* at the café brushes my hand with a smile as he passes me my morning cappuccino. The shopkeeper who bundles up my postcards gives me a wink. At dinner, a *cameriere* pulls out a chair for me whispering "*Buona sera, signora,*" in a low sensuous voice, keeping a firm hand on my back.

When I return to Los Angeles and report these flirtations to my husband, he laughs it off with, "Unbelievable! That stuff was beat out of us guys in the seventies. I held open a door for a woman once back then and she read me the riot act. And now with sexual harassment, I could be sued for reckless eyeballing if I turn my head towards a female for two seconds longer than I'm *supposed to* at work."

I ask him to stare at me and he gives it a try, but it just results in mutual giggles. Decades-long marriages and the enticing mysteries of the flirting game go together like a bowl of minestrone topped with tiramisu.

So I go to Italy and play the soft, subtle version of the game, now that I've grown from *signorina* to *signora*, knowing the strategy is to not take any of it seriously. It's a harmless way to get a little lift, simply accepting being appreciated for nothing more than being a woman.

Walking along Rome's Via del Corso there's so much to admire—from the guy with the slicked back hair and leather jacket speeding along on his moto who brings back memories of bad-boy high school heartthrobs, to the elegant set who stroll

7

with their suit jackets slung behind them off their index fingers, displaying tempting torsos in crisp white shirts. Mix these visions with church bell gongs, gushing fountains, naked thick-rippling-muscled statues and a street violinist playing *Besame Mucho* and I am oh-so relaxed as we catch each other's eyes.

I realize my style differs from how other American women play it when I sit with Mario, a bar owner in Positano. Suddenly, a table of American women of a certain age, having had one too many limoncellos, zig-zags by to give Mario their *buona nottes*. One of them, a bleached blonde, squeezed into white jeans with silver studded pockets, turns to present her rear to Mario. He pats and pinches obligingly, sending her giggling away. As soon as she's out the door he throws up his hands, "Aagghh! American women! They don't understand the affair is an affair. The European woman, she knows it's just what it is, she can take care of herself, and let us men be. But these Americans!"

Fabio, a handsome, deeply tanned boatman, joins in: "I'm exhausted. All summer I bring the American women from here to Capri. We have the sun, the wine… Then one of them has a top off, another one a bottom off. I am a man, what can I do? But it's too much, too much—they come here, they expect!"

Back in Rome, the trend becomes even more obvious when I walk by a Piazza Navona caffe and see a group of females ogling a businessman in a well-tailored suit. He puts his head down, avoiding entanglement. It all adds up to the inverse of Ruth Orkin's masterpiece. Now it's The Italian Boy In Italy who's being leered at by gangs of American women.

Ladies, please stop!

Is this behavior going to ruin my game? Will the cougars with their blatant expectations scare off the *signori*? I have an urge to start a campaign to end this, like the Italians did when a McDonalds was opened beneath the Spanish Steps and they started the Slow Food Movement to preserve the country's culinary culture. Their symbol is the snail, posted on all establishments that play by Slow Food rules.

I imagine plastering Rome with symbols of the Italian Stare, setting up enclaves where none of this breed of American woman tourists can trespass, so the delicate tradition can be preserved safely, and these men won't become an endangered species.

I finish up my glass of wine and turn to look at the staring *signor*. He raises an eyebrow to add just the right mischievous element. It's as if he's beckoning words from the Roman poet Ovid's advice to men in the *Art of Love*: "They may cry, naughty, but they want to be overcome..."

Could he be the one who slung me over his shoulder in the Forum those many years ago?

"Buona notte," I say to him, as I head out the door, tossing my scarf over my shoulder.

Now in the Roman night, I realize the shock that rocked my world 30 years ago has transformed to a flutter, that whispers enchantingly:

We are men, you are women. We are alive! And what a fun game we play!

****

Advice for Rome Wine Bars:

L'Angolo Divino (Via dei Balestrari 12, closed Monday), is where this story takes place. The name translates to "Divine Corner"—perfect for this warm, candlelit spot that's just steps away from the Campo dei Fiori hub-bub. Owner

Massimo has an extensive wine collection, and is always helpful for your selections. Besides delicious servings of cheeses and salumi, you can get a good light meal here.

Cantina Lucifero (www.cantinalucifero.it, Via del Pellegrino 53), is a tiny, cozy spot, also near the Campo dei Fiori, that along with a wonderful wine selection, serves northern Italian specialties, such as fondue.

Cul de Sac (www.enotecaculdesac.com, Piazza di Pasquino 73)**,** has been around since Rome's wine bar boom began in the 1970s, with a list of 1500 choices. Get there before 9 to score an outside table, with a view of one of Rome's "talking statues"=Pasquino, where rants about current events are posted. Small plates here are delicious classics, including involtini alla Romana (rolled stuffed veal), and they have excellent house made pates.

Enoteca Provincia Romana, (www.enotecaprovinciaromana.it,

Foro Traiano 82-84), is a great stop after a visit to the Forum, where you can wind down in chic surroundings, with a view of Trajan's Column, and enjoy food and wine from the province of Rome. Check out their website for happy hours and events.

Letters from Italy

*A fun way to get to know Rome's Wine Bars is to join a
Wine Bar Walk with* **Context Travel:**
www.contexttravel.com

Letter from Rome:
Get Me To A Nunnery

I confess: All my life I've been prone to Girl Crushes—that intense attraction to another female. For me it takes the shape of "You are so beautiful to me…can I BE you for just one day?" These days, my short list includes Nancy Pelosi, Patti Smith, and Sylvia Poggioli.

The Crushes began with Nuns. Growing up in the sixties there was much inspiration—Julie Andrews romping through the Alps in the "Sound of Music," Sally Field getting airborne every Thursday night in "The Flying Nun."

Closer in was my beloved Catechism teacher, Sister Ann: a full-moon-faced beauty in a long black habit, with her clickety-clackety rosary bead belt, swishing through the classroom aisles in a perfume cloud of faint frankincense. Sister Ann had the power to terrify us eight-year old First Communion students, sweetly telling the story about the little boy who skipped mass, went fishing, drowned, and was dragged down to burn in hell. Or she'd send a thrilling rush through me as she pressed a gold star into my Catechism book, nodding her head with a beatific smile, after I'd successfully recited my perfectly memorized *Act of Contrition*.

Sister Ann's focus was teaching us "to avoid the near occasion of sin," in the words of that *Act of Contrition*. She told us our souls had been purified by baptism, but in our eight years of life, God had been watching our every move and tallying black marks on our pure white centers. I knew I had many sinful thoughts and deeds. I trembled in the confessional, whispering to Father Gary behind the smoky glass. Oh how heartfully sorry I was for cheating at Go Fish, stealing Milky Ways from my brother's Halloween candy stash, and calling my baby sister Stinky.

I figured I could put an end to all these scary thoughts about my misdeeds with one simple move: I'd become a nun. I'd follow every mysterious ritual perfectly, be constantly good, and certainly go straight to heaven. Maybe I'd even fly. Maybe Christopher Plummer would ask me to marry him. I practiced the costume before bed--pulling my stretchy top up over my head, arranging it around my face like a habit. Then I'd hold my hands in solemn prayer and pace the hallway, until my mother would march me into bed, where terrifying thoughts of my sinfulness would keep me awake in the darkness.

It didn't take long before I discovered a hitch in my nun plan: the vow of celibacy. I was crazy over the neighbor boy Billy, and no way was I going to give up my favorite part of our play times: kissing him bye-bye behind the shed. So I took a step away to admire the Brides of Jesus from afar. I fantasized about what life was like for them behind their convent door. *Did they watch The Flying Nun? Did they have color TV?* I'd stand in awe when I'd see them at the Shop-Rite, buying chickens at the counter, packing their bags into their station wagon, and driving away. *Did they fight over who would pull the wishbone of that chicken?*

Over the decades the fascination stuck, filling me with wonder each time I spot a nun. Not that I see nuns very much here in Los Angeles. But in Rome they are everywhere. Strolling through the piazzas. Eating gelato. Buying panties at the shop around the corner from the Campo dei Fiori market. On a Wednesday Papal audience at the Vatican I was surrounded by gangs of them—clambering over each other to stand on chairs, as if they were at a rock concert, waving their arms, shouting, "Papa! Papa! Viva Papa!"

It's a thrill to be in the midst of these floating holy women, or "*suore*" as the Italians call them. They're all decked out in crisp habits—white, brown, navy. My favorites are the Brigattines—a Swedish order, uniformed in long gray, with tight headpieces accented by a white band and red studs. On my perfectly timed days, I stop by their church on the Piazza Farnese in the late afternoons, where they gather to sing vespers in sweet harmonies. Runners up are the Pious Disciples of the Divine Master (*aka* the PDDM sisters), who dress in pale blue. They kneel in the front pews of Saint Peter's Chapel of the Blessed Sacrament, silently devoting prayers to the Eucharist.

As I gravitate towards nuns, Italians pull me away. "They're bad luck," says my friend Mario, practically tearing my arm off when we're strolling down Via Corso and he spots a *suora* coming towards us. Apparently passing a nun to many

Italians (Mario included), is like having a black cat cross your path. To ward off the evil, they "tocca ferro"—touch iron. And since iron is not readily available, Italian men touch their balls. Then to totally insure the spell hasn't landed on them, they say to the next stranger walking by, *"Suora Tua"*="Your nun"—or the shortened version: *"Tua"*—to pass the curse along.

In 1999, a trio of young Italian nuns, sick of being shunned by the Italian citizenry, rose up in protest. They recorded an album, *"Suora Tua-Tocca Ferro"* to dispel the superstition. The song got some play, but did nothing to dispell the centuries old nun-avoiding tradition.

Which is why Mario is dismayed when I tell him I've booked myself for a stay in Rome's Fraterna Domus. It's a convent that offers simple, cheap, guest rooms.

"You must take this with you," he says, stuffing one of his prized possessions into my purse. It's a *corno*—or what we in New Jersey called "an Italian horn"--one of those curvy red pepper charms, that's supposed to ward off evil.

"Nothing bad is going to happen," I say. "It'll be heavenly."

***

17

I'm hit with the smell of thick, swampy holy water as soon as the Fraterna Domus door opens. Standing before me is a prim, pixie-haired *signora*, dressed in a blue sweater and matching skirt. She reaches out her hand to introduce herself: "Sister Milena."

The bad luck has begun. I've landed in a convent run by Lay Sisters who don't wear habits, and habits are an essential fetish of my girl-crush. If I saw this Milena or any of her kind walking on the street, I wouldn't even suspect she'd taken the poverty, chastity, obedience vow. Mario wouldn't even "Tocca Ferro" We'd just think she shopped at Talbot's.

As Milena's sidekick, Sister Cecilia, checks me in, I struggle to tame the scolding tone out of my voice and ask, "So...why don't you wear habits?" It turns out the skirt/sweater ensembles are the whole point, they *want* to blend in. "We are an order that began in 1969, to help the poor," Sister Cecilia says. "We're not different from the people we help, so we don't want to dress differently from them." Drat. I had hoped she'd answer that their nun wear was at the dry cleaners, and they'd be getting it right that very afternoon.

Adding to the letdown is the convent décor: Simple knotty pine furnishings, wood block paintings, plastic daisies. You'd think a tad of that splendid Baroque that covers all the surrounding churches would have seeped in here. But clearly their designer was going for a Post Vatican II look, circa 1970s, when simple brown was so very "in."

My room is a basement cell: Ikea-style furniture, white walls. There's a high window that's street level, covered up with a grate. The closet sized bathroom is one of those old fashioned set-ups I've experienced in Italian 2-star hotels: no shower separation——a sprayer hangs from the ceiling, and water drains out holes in the floor. Wisely, the nuns added a toilet paper cover to keep it dry——nice touch. And there's a spigot sticking out of the toilet, so it can double as a bidet. Not that I would even think of touching myself down there in such a place as this.

I sigh over a cute embroidered towel with a Fraterna Domus emblem on it, tempted to snitch it. And then turn to see a friendly looking Jesus hanging over my little bed...*Oh, save me from the near occasion of sin.* This Jesus is a particularly handsome interpretation, with long hair, goatee, and moustache. White boxers. Neat red, spidery lines spurt from his hands and feet, matching the color of my bedspread. *What does this Jesus look like to Bride of Jesus Sister Milena...Does she see him and think—that's my husband, who suffered for every sin of mankind?* I reach up to touch the cross, and it tilts off the nail into my hand. *Hmm...easily removable if it gets too distracting.*

"Susanna?" I jump at the sound of a chirpy voice behind me. I'd left the door open, and turn to see Sister Milena, eyebrows raised to her hairline. In full panic, I make an idiot move to hook cross to nail. It lands crookedly, and Sister Milena swoops in to straighten it.

"It fell," I lie...*Lying about Jesus to a nun!*

A nervous laugh escapes from me. Sister Milena purses her lips and hands me my passport—that I'd forgotten upstairs when I'd checked in. I thank her, clumsily stuffing it into my purse, so clumsily that Mario's red *corno* slips out. The *corno* lands on the floor, between our feet. It seems to have grown since Mario handed it to me, the naughty red pagan object lying there as if it's about to burst into flames, dragging me down to Hell. I have an urge to stomp on it, but I'm frozen, head bowed. Sister Milena glances down, clucks, gives me a mysterious smile, turns, and walks away in silence.

I stand in the doorway speechless, heart pounding. Even without the habit, these "suore" have The Power Over Me. I shrink back to my eight year old self, covered in that heavenly ache only a girl crush can deliver.

****

Advice about Rome Convent Stays:

This story takes place at **Fraterna Domus, www.fraternadomus.it** (Via Monte Brianzo, 62, (39) 06-688-02727, fraternadomus@alice.it, Curfew: 11pm).

Lunch and dinners served here are very good and a bargain. Even if you haven't booked a room, you can call and make a reservation.

Some other convents I've stayed in:

Casa di Santa Brigida, www.brigidine.org (Piazza Farnese 96, (39) 06-688-92596, piazzafarnese@brigidine.org)

This wins for best location (right on the Piazza Farnese), and the best dressed nuns in Rome. Saint Brigid from Sweden lived here in the 14th century, and her library and downstairs rooms are beautifully appointed. Guest rooms are simple and comfy and there's a rooftop terrace. You have to reserve way in advance here, as this is one of the best bargains in the historic center.

There are loads of good restaurants surrounding you, including the fancy **Camponeschi:** (Piazza Farnese, 39 0668 74927, www.ristorantecamponeschi.it, closed Sun) and the budget **Ai Balestrari:** (Via dei Balestrari 41, 39 0668 5377, www.balestrari.it, closed Mon).

Casa di Santa Francesca Romana,

www.sfromana.it, Via dei Vascellari 61, (39) 06-5812125, istituto@sfromana.it, No curfew)

This is actually a training center for priests, so you won't see nuns here. It's wonderfully located in Trastevere, near the Basilica di Santa Cecilia. The breakfast buffet is abundant and delicious. There's a chapel, and lots of photos and paintings of popes and cardinals. The building was once the home of Francesca Buzza, who dedicated her life to helping the poor and sick, and performed miracles. She died here in 1608 and was canonized as Santa Francesca Romana, co-patron saint of Rome.

Santa Sofia, www.casasantasofia.it (Piazza della Madonna dei Monti 3, (39) 06 485-778, info@casasantasofia.it, No Curfew)

An order of Russian Orthodox nuns runs this simple spot, in the under-touristed Monti neighborhood, near the Colosseum. They wear habits (hoorah!) and sing in sweet harmonies at mass in the church next door. There are great budget-friendly restaurants in the neighborhood, including **Taverna Romana** (Via Madonna dei Monti 79, 39 06-474-5325, Closed Tues), and **La Barrique** (Via del Boschetto 41, 39 06 4782 5953).

For more info:

American Church in Rome's Santa Susanna website: www.santasusanna.org

Monastery Stays in Italy: www.monasterystays.com

Postcard From Rome: The Legend of La Befana

"There is no Santa Claus in Italy," my Nana told me when I was a kid. I had nightmares of how awful Christmas must be over there. Nana said she had to wait until January 6, The Feast of the Epiphany, to get gifts. The presents came from an old crone with a hairy mole on her chin who rode around on a broom. She was called *La Befana*.

Many years later, I'm in Rome's Piazza Navona, at the Epiphany Fair. It's two weeks after Christmas, but the holiday celebration is still in full swing. Bernini's Fountain of the Four Rivers is surrounded by stands covered in twinkling white lights, selling sweets, ornaments, and roasted pork sandwiches.

Nowadays, there is Santa Claus in Italy. They call him *Babbo Natale*. Figures of him (skinnier than our version) hang off the booths. But he's far outnumbered by *La Befanas*—that witch of my childhood nightmares. There's no escaping her in the piazza—she appears in the form of thimble-sized clay totems, stuffed dolls with scary grins, and there's even a *signora* in costume, cackling and waving her broom at Italian *bambini* who look up at her in awe.

Tonight, January 5, I tell my husband, is La Befana's special night.

"The HORROR," he whispers.

Actually, once you get to know the Legend of La Befana, you might warm up to her.

La Befana, like my Nana, was famous for spending her days in the kitchen, cooking and sweeping. On the first Christmas, the Magi stopped by her house, asking directions to Bethlehem. She made them dinner and they told her, "We're going to see the Christ child, want to come along?" "Impossible," she replied. "There are all these dishes to wash and the kitchen to sweep!" So the kings went on their way. Then, as the old woman was sweeping, it hit her: *Did those guys say they were going to see Jesus?*

She ran out of her cottage with her broom to follow them, but... no kings in sight. She kept running, until her broom lifted her into the air. Ever since, La Befana has flown through the night sky on the Eve of the Epiphany, delivering goodies to children, hoping one of them is the Christ child.

Anticipation is in the Piazza Navona air, as kids hurry home to hang stockings and set out a glass of wine for La Befana. She knows no child has been perfect all year, so tomorrow morning they'll find their stockings filled with a mix of treats: coal (actually delicious black rock candy), maybe onions, olive oil... and finally they'll dig to the bottom and find chocolates and caramels.

Who could not adore this ordinary woman, caught in the midst of her ordinary world, suddenly struck by The Epiphany, dropping everything to run and be a part of it?

I flash on my friends in Los Angeles, who have already hauled their trees out to the curb and are back at work, feeling guilty about weight they've gained from holiday partying.

We don't feel guilty at all. We're in Rome and we do as the Romans do. We slip into Tre Scalini, and order tartufo—crunchy chocolate ice cream encrusted in hard chocolate.

The nightmares Nana gave me so long ago are gone. We buy our Los Angeles friends Befanas, wanting to share with them the spirit of this Christmastime bonus; wanting them to believe as Italians believe, as we believe: that La Befana will fly through the sky tonight, sweeping away last year's troubles with her broom, bringing us the hope of a sweeter, brighter new year. Anything is possible.

****

Christmas in Rome Advice:

It's lovely to spend Christmas time in Rome or anywhere in Italy.

The season officially begins on **December 8, the Feast of the Immaculate Conception**. In Rome, the Pope places a wreath over a statue of the Madonna that sits high up on a column at **Piazza Mignanelli**, near the Spanish Steps.

Churches are filled with
Nativity scenes=*Presepe*.
Zampognari=bagpipe players serenade piazza
visitors.

Traditional sweets are **panettone** (plain cake
flavored with dry fruits), **pandoro** (simple star-
shaped cake, often served with cream or nutella),
and **torrone** (nougat candy).

Since Christmas is a family holiday, many
restaurants are closed. It's best to plan ahead with
reservations—if you're up to splurge, check out
hotels that offer special mid-day dinners, such as
Hotel de Russie (www.hotelderussie.it). Also, the
Tavole Romane blog, www.tavoleromane.it,
written by Roman foodies, can give you up-to-date
suggestions for Christmas and New Year's Eve
dinners.

Don't miss **Midnight Mass on Christmas Eve**,
when churches are filled with wonderful music. If
you can take the crowds, you can stand in St.
Peter's square to see the Pope's Midnight Mass on
Jumbotrons, or get there **Christmas Day** when he
appears outside at noon for his **"Urbi et Orbi"**
(of the city of Rome and the world) blessing.

December 26 is La Festa di San Stefano, so there are more celebrations in St. Peter's square and many places are closed.

Lots of restaurants offer **fixed price New Year's Eve dinners**--again check out **Tavole Romane's blog: www.tavoleromane.com** for suggestions. Reserve in advance and you'll find yourself deliciously welcoming in the New Year, toasting with prosecco and celebrating with the traditional good luck dish of lentils to bring on prosperity.

You'll be hearing lots of "Buon Natale, Buon Anno, and Auguri=Best Wishes" all the way through to **The Feast of the Epiphany of January 6**...and even the days after can be lovely and relaxing, as Italians slowly recover from their splendid holiday weeks.

Letter from Pisa:
The Accidental Tour Guide

"Wow, getta load of the way these Italian women walk in spike-heeled boots," a woman whispers, as I, *That Woman in the Spike-Heeled Boots*, make my way down the aisle of a train headed for Pisa.

"*Scusi, signora,*" says a *ragazzo* in a *Zucchero* t-shirt, as he offers to lift my wheelie up to a rack.

"*Grazie,*" I smile, taking a seat. Cheers explode inside of me: *Brava, they think you're one of them!*

Oh, how I love playing my "I'm an Italian game."

Thank you, blessed DNA from my maternal line that's given me this dark wavy hair and the bootie that's a bit on the big side for Los Angeles, but fits perfectly in *bell'Italia*. Thank you *signoras* for teaching me by your example the look I've finally mastered after traveling here for years: big sunglasses, scarf tied "just-so," sexy yet functional footwear.

A plump senior citizen *signora*, with a Madonna medallion bouncing between her breasts, takes a seat across from me. As the train begins to chug along, she nods me a kind *Buon Giorno* and then opens up a white paper bag, offering me a true Tuscan treasure: a *pignole* cookie. I've been loving these cookies every single day of this trip. They're heaven sent: light and chewy, studded with pine nuts that fall from the trees around here like manna.

Bless you *Signora of the Pignole* cookies. We smile at each other as we nibble and watch the hills go by.

Across the aisle I notice a quiet American couple, passing a guidebook back and forth. *Aggh, that guidebook, that drek I'd read in Los Angeles when I was planning my trip to Pisa.* Nothing in there but the standard ho-hum about the main attraction. In brief it says: *Pisa, Rush in, snap photo of you and your mate holding up the tower for future slide show, climb tower, buy postcard, cross off list, then get outta town! Pisa is the Queen of Tourist Quickies!*

I am not the Tourist-Quickie type, especially when it comes to Italian travel.

A couple of weeks before this train ride, I'd landed at the Pisa airport and tossed that guidebook aside. My take was to turn the Tourist-Quickie situation into a positive. I figured if Pisa had only one "must see" attraction, the pressure's off. It'd be completely different from Rome or Venice, with so many "must sees", that when I touch down an immediate restlessness takes over.

I arrived in Pisa agenda-free, hopped in a cab at the town's tiny airport, and twenty minutes later, was at my lovely Royal Victoria Hotel. Right across the *via* was the River Arno. It was sunset and the sky was putting on its quintessential Tuscan twilight show, complete with rosy streaked clouds and golden rays. I watched a pair of nuns cross the river's pale stone bridge. The nuns eclipsed a pair of lovers at the center of the bridge who fell into an embrace and a long romantic kiss. Students glided by on bikes. *Signoras* in fashionable wool suits walked arm in arm. Church bells rang. The *passegiata*--the early evening stroll! My entrée into Jetlagger's Heaven: Pisa!

I easily slipped into the stroll, eat, nap rhythms of the perfect Italian vacation, and discovered outside Pisa's Tourist Quickie zone, there's a real-live-enchanting medieval town. So I stuck with the local action—indulged in long lunches at cozy trattorias stuffing myself with homemade *tagliatelle*, wandered through cobblestoned streets, quiet Romanesque churches, took guilt free afternoon naps, drank wine on the rooftop of my hotel to watch more of those sunsets. And sure, on the last day I joined the tourists and marveled over The Campo dei Miracoli and the Tower.

I'd gone on from Pisa to southern Tuscany to help friends out with an olive harvest and now was feeling all blended in with Italy, wrapping up my trip with a return to My Pisa and the Royal Victoria.

The train stops and away goes *La Signora of the Pignole Cookies*, wishing me a *"Buona giornata"*. I watch her waddle across the platform to meet what must be her daughter. The two double-cheek kiss, daughter takes the *pignole*, and they fade away to what I imagine will be a beautiful lunch.

I'm left alone. And there, across the aisle from me they sit, beginning to haunt me: that 70-something year old guidebook couple. He's a Jack

Klugman look-alike, so I'll call him Jack. And she's small and bird-boned, like one of the Pigeon sisters from the odd Couple, so she shall be called Cecily.

I know a chef who says that for him watching people eating bad food is a form of torture. I have the same reaction to watching people traveling badly in Italy.

I look around to see if I can change my seat. As I swivel, Cecily catches my eye. And smiles.

Oh, the poor dears need me... I lean in:

"Going to Pisa?"

Cecily and Jack bolt back: "You're American?!"

My nod is part confessional, part "thank you for appreciating my performance."

Jack is off and running, "Yep, we're going to Pisa, going to see that tower." Partner Cecily provides visual aid, by waving that guidebook in my face.

Kismet. I was put on this train at this moment to become for this couple "That mah-velous woman we met on the train to Pisa who turned a day trip into a fah-bulous memory."

Me: "I know some great restaurants you can go to for lunch."

Jack: "Oh no, we're just going to see the tower and then get back on the train to Florence."

Now is when it would be handy to have my husband by my side to translate Jack's line into: "Shut up." But without him there, I'm off, the bubbliest of restaurant reviewers, babbling on about how *favoloso* the bistecca is at Hotel Orologio, or maybe they'd like the *tagliatelle* at Osteria Cavalieri. "Wait until you walk into these places—the smell of truffles hits you as soon as you open the door—they're in season and they're shaving them on EVERYTHING!"

I stop to take a breath and see I've lost half my audience. Cecily has her nose buried back in that guidebook. Jack's still with me. But those glazed over eyes tell all. He's simply playing the part in the deal they've struck up over their 50-plus years of marriage, "Honey, you take care of the nuisance, will you?"

An out of body experience is in play. There's another me out there heckling, "Put a sock in it! They don't care!" But my Good Samaritan compulsion is unstoppable.

I switch from food to Pisa attractions to win Cecily back. I charge into raves about the treasures of the Borgo Stretto, the arched walkway in the old city, with that Salza 1898 caffe that whisks you back a hundred years and serves those homemade chocolates. Or if they wanted something quieter, there's the stroll along the Arno, where they could stop by the gothic Santa Maria della Spina, a mini-masterpiece I visited on a rainy morning, with water rushing through the mouths of its rooftop gargoyles.

Cecily makes a show out of checking her watch, obviously grateful that the arrival time for Pisa is near and they'll soon shake me.

Fine, I think, turning away to gather up my things. Go ahead and do your "been-there-done-that." I won't warn you what you'll get when you visit the world's most popular architectural mistake. That TOWER you've seen in pictures all your lives is actually a bit of a disappointment--at only eight stories. And you wanna know what it looks like these days? The leaning two-bottom tiers of scaffolding, that's what.

And The Campo dei Miracoli--that "glorious grassy piazza that surrounds the Tower, Baptistery, Duomo, and Campo Santo" you've just read about? If you hit it now, it'll be mobbed by sloppy tourists milling about with their video cameras. It's so much prettier at sunset! And you really should visit the Campo Santo—the amazing cemetery, with those beautiful frescoes...*aaggh*, I know you'll miss them like almost everyone does.

Go ahead, climb the tower like I did. Circle up 300 steps with a family from Colorado, complete with two elementary school aged boys—their yelps echoing along with the reconstruction whines of metal drills against stone, dad bringing up the rear cursing that the batteries in his camera are wearing down, mom getting vertigo...

The train pulls into the Pisa station. I reach for my bag and the *ragazzo* in the Zucchero t-shirt approaches: "I 'elp you," he says, smirking. I'm deflating... *I blew my I'm An Italian Signora cover for those ungrateful two and now the whole train knows my secret.*

As I wheel my suitcase towards the exit, I nod a farewell to Jack and Cecily. The look they give me stops me in my tracks. It's unmistakably a look of pity: *Aw, you poor dear solo woman who can't shut up...*

Wait a minute: *I started my whole conversation with you because I pitied you, and now...*

I blast out cheerfulness to set them straight: "We could share a cab. My hotel's on the way to the tower!"

Cecily clutches her purse and Jack gives me a stern, "No, no, that won't be necessary," as they bust away to an opposite exit.

When I see them two people down from me in the taxi line, out comes my final flail at a mahvelous impression, "*Ciao, buon viaggio!*" Cecily turns away and Jack's panicked wave clearly reads more like, "Go away!" then "*Arrivederci.*"

Face it: I've transformed in their eyes from Italian *signora* to pesky American traveler to pitiful blabbering solo woman to some crook they expect to read about as "Italy's Latest Traveler's Scam": *Beware the lone woman who appears helpful. She'll offer great restaurant advice, but she's actually in cahoots with a local cabbie. She'll get you in a taxi and then they'll both rob you blind!*

On the cab ride back to my hotel I play my misbehavior back in my head, audibly *aaggh-ing.*

At times like these I often find it helpful to blame others. A list begins to take shape: guidebook writers, tour companies, all those Tourist-Quickie encouragers of the world. Moving on, I could always blame my parents for having me as the middle child—a position in the pecking order that's always made me extra-needy for attention.

What about all those tedious warnings caring friends always gave me about solo woman travelers: *"Carry a money belt, pay the extra price to stay at a safe hotel, avoid dark alleys…"* Why didn't they include something like: "Be aware that at times… such as when one has been three weeks picking olives with natives and struggling with her pidgin Italian and sign language, the opportunity to finally speak in one's native tongue to fellow travelers may make you go over the top and become…*Insufferable.*

Ouch. I changed the channel with the no-fail Italian cure: food. A delicious lunch of *tagliatelle* and *porcini.* Two glasses of Chianti. Then instead of heading for the traditional nap, I realized I had to get a souvenir for my nephew and only something tower-related would do. So I headed back to Tourist Quickie central: the Campo dei Miracoli.

After doling out too many euros for an ugly pennant, I curved toward the tower for a final look. And there he was: Jack, frantically waving for a cab, all of which at lunchtime were lined up driverless. I knew he saw me by the look of alarm

40

on his face. And there was Cecily two steps behind him, equally appalled. My appearance was the perfect end to their movie: like Glenn Close rising from the bathtub in *Fatal Attraction.*

I could have told Jack the drivers would be back in 15 minutes after they'd finished their lunch break. But instead I went along with his "we don't see each other" game.

That's right, Jack. That scene on the train with the American woman, that never happened.

What you see is an Italian *signora* in spike-heeled boots, turning away, walking back to the old city, slipping into a bakery to buy *pignole* cookies, greeting the shopkeeper with a *buona sera,* as the church bells ring.

****

Beyond the Leaning Tower of Pisa Advice:

Stay a while in Jetlagger's Heaven. Pisa's airport is a small, stress-free entry point to Tuscany, and a short cab ride to the pleasures of the historic center.

Hotels:

Royal Victoria Hotel, (www.royalvictoria.it, 12 Lungarno Pacinotti Tel. (+39) 050.940.111) This 3-star hotel has been owned and managed by the Piegaja family since 1837, and became a favorite spot for travelers on The Grand Tour. It's a sprawling property, combining a medieval tower and 16ᵗʰ century buildings, featuring spacious salons, antique furnishings, and a rooftop terrace to enjoy the sunset. The staff and breakfast buffet are wonderful.

Hotel Relais dell'Orologio,

(www.hotelrelaisorologio.com, Via della Faggiola 12/14, 39 050 830361) Pisa's only 5-star hotel is a former 14ᵗʰ century tower house that's been masterfully renovated in Baroque-chic style, retaining original Renaissance frescoes. The restaurant, with a garden for alfresco dining, is divine.

Eat:

Osteria dei Cavalieri,

(www.osteriacavallieri.pisa.it, Via San Frediano 16, 39 050/580858, Closed Saturday afternoon and Sunday, and in August) A warm, welcoming restaurant to enjoy fine wines and delicious Pisan specialties, such as ravioli (filled with pecorino, tomatoes, and beans) or grilled bistecca and porcini.

Osteria dei Mille, (Via dei Mille 30/32, 050/556263) A beloved by locals place, not far from The Tower that serves traditional Tuscan fare and fantastic homemade pastas.

Vineria alla Piazza, (Piazza Vettovaglie, 39 050 3820433, Cash only, Closed Sundays) This casual, Slow Food restaurant, right on Pisa's daily market square, changes its menu daily according to what's in season. A great place to enjoy delicious homemade pasta and salads with the locals.

Salza dal 1898, (www.salza.it, Borgo Stretto 46, Closed Mondays) Treat yourself to a caffe and homemade chocolate or pastry at this elegant old world oasis on Pisa's pedestrian only shopping street.

Il Vecchio Forno, (Via Cavalca) THE bakery to stock up on traditional cantucci and pignole.

Paul DeBondt Chocolate,
(www.debondtchocolate.com, Lungarno Pacinotti 5) Artisan Paul DeBondt is a major player on the new, booming Tuscan chocolate scene. Stop by this simple, modern shop to indulge in his rich, unique creations.

Letter from Venice:
Pasta is Dead!

"Pasta is dead! Long live sculpted meat!" was the battle cry of the leader of the Italian Futurist Movement, Fillipo Tommaso Martinetti. Hearing this cockamamie slogan, I imagine *nonnas* wailing as caskets of spaghetti are wheeled through *vias*, while renegade Martinetti sculpts a pile of ground meat into a Brancusi-esque figure. In fact, when Martinetti shouted out his manifesto in 1932, Neapolitans rose up in protest, with their mayor shouting back, "Vermicelli with tomato sauce is the food of angels!" To which Martinetti replied, "That confirms it: life in paradise is a bore."

Seriously? This is what I'm learning at the Gritti Hotel's School of Fine Cooking in Venice.

I've landed here smack on the one day of the year when the class topic is Futurism—that early twentieth century movement created by hot heads who wanted Italy to "get with" the Industrial Age. With Mussolini's support, Martinetti rallied allies in the north to promote locally grown rice as the national dish. Futurists believed it was all pasta's fault that Italy was in the dark ages—according to them, it caused lethargy, nostalgic inactivity, and certainly was not the food of heroes.

Sigh... This nine in the morning lecture is not jiving with my Venetian dreams. *Ah, La Serenissima--the most serene--the nickname Italians have given to this magical place.* I'm in what must be the most gorgeous classroom on the planet, all pastels, curlicue gold picture frames, and curvy candelabras.

In 1525 Doge Andrea Gritti had this palazzo built for his family. Its frothy grandeur delighted me from the moment I wheeled in my suitcase, alongside my traveling galfriend Mary.

That was yesterday afternoon, and now I am nursing the Hangover of all Hangovers. First came the welcoming bottle of prosecco, that Mary and I popped as we jumped around the suite fit for a contessa, ecstatic that it had two marble bathrooms. Then there was the toasting on our terrace, while the twilight hour began. As I unpacked, Mary grabbed the Gritti Hotel Libro D'Oro (Gold Book), reading aloud names of guests who came before us, as we imagined them all here at once: Pavarotti and Mick Jagger, Orson Welles and Woody Allen, Elizabeth Taylor and Shirley Temple. And of course Hemingway, who famously threw his empties from his balcony into the canal.

With our prosecco bottle emptied, the next logical step was to charge out into the starlit night and hit some *bacari*=wine bars. Here's where memory begins to blur. There was that spot near San Marco where a pint-sized *signor* in a tweed suit made a grab for my bottom. Then came the inevitable: whenever I am traveling with Mary, her cute curvy body and long blonde braid make men bark. Sure enough, a native seaman named Beppe fell under her spell. Off we went with him guiding us over bridges, through dark alleys, hitting hidden places where only the locals go, drinking enough prosecco to wash an elephant.

Now I'm in class, guzzling Pellegrino, wishing I could attach a hose to the bottle and flush out my booze-soaked insides. I'm at the English speaker's table, surrounded by two doe-eyed 30-something banker gals from Boston, a couple of Dutch ladies and Anna, a dour translator *signora*. The rest of the room is full of glamorous Venetians, decked out in Prada ensembles, looking as though they've just stepped off the pages of Italian *Vogue*. I'm dressed in black Eileen Fisher. It looked chic in the Los Angeles Bloomingdale's dressing room. But compared to the locals, I might as well be wrapped in a potato sack, with my front teeth blacked out and hair in hillbilly braids.

Since I understand Italian, I'm getting the Futurist lecture in disturbing stereo—first from the droning scholar and then in English from translator Anna. *Futurism*...I flip through the photos of recipes in my class folder, and the dishes look no different from what I could order back home at Spago in Beverly Hills. *Damn you Martinetti! I came to Venice for all the traditional stuff I've craved—pasta with anchovy sauce, creamed baccala...*

But instead, we're being schooled about Martinetti's Futurist restaurant, The Holy Palate, that he opened in Turin in 1931. He set it up so guests ate without utensils to "experience" small portions of food, as he believed Futurists must eat light "so the body is ready for artistic invention." While customers nibbled using their right hands, they'd be offered textures to stroke on their left, such as sandpaper or velvet. In celebration of the Industrial Age, sounds of airplane engines were blasted in the background, as waiters sprayed diners' heads with carnation perfume.

No one is laughing or even smirking, copious notes are being scribbled around me. This whole furious Futurism talk is bringing me back to San Francisco Punk Rock days, when I slam danced to the Sex Pistols, reveling in "Destruction is the highest form of creation" anthems. And *aaagghh, my head aches.* Made worse when Chef Turco appears and flips on a food processor to puree cauliflower—a jackhammer on my fragile nerves.

I drop my pen and call up a skill I perfected in high school algebra class: pretend to pay attention while drifting to my own soundtrack... *Yes, drift as smoothly as a gondola under the Bridge of Sighs... put on Vivaldi's "Four Seasons"...that traditional stand-by he wrote while living here in calmer times...*

Chef Turco is *molto bello*, a Hugh Grant look-alike, with even better long-lashed peepers. Thankfully, he's not sculpting meat, but making a pretty plate of monkfish scallops with his delicate hands.

I drift along with the group to the Gritti's Longhi bar, where Futurist cocktails await: gin flavored with licorice, served in martini glasses, with a mini-scroll of the Futurist Manifesto and cherry tomato on top. "Don't eat the tomato," says translator Anna, "it's just symbolic, to be thrown away, like the tradition of tomato sauce on pasta." But it's too late, I've already popped it, and pushed the glass of liquor away. *Take that, Martinetti!*

On to the splendid dining room, where fortunately waiters do not spray our heads with carnation perfume. We lunch on Chef Turco's creations, his Futurist style being more like nouvelle, and quite delicious.

"Buonissimo," I say to the fancy Venetian lady sitting next to me.

"*Si,*" she nods, and then whispers, "But I would never make it for my husband." *Aha, did you hear that, Martinetti? I've even got a northern Italian on my side!*

The terrace just out the door is too much to resist. I slip away during dessert to take in the soft cool air and the Grand Canal view: the white domed Santa Maria della Salute Church across the way. Miraculously, my head is clearing.

Had Martinetti seen me so blissful over this traditional sight, he would have drop-kicked me off this dock. But, lucky for me, his Futurism had no future. Pasta did not die, *La Serenissima* lives on. So I could stand there, fully content, immersed in its timeless beauty.

****

Some Venice Advice:

Gritti Palace Hotel, (www.thegrittipalace.com**,** Campo Santa Maria del Giglio, 2467, 041 296 1222) A magical, luxurious place to stay in Venice. And even if you're not sleeping there, have a Bellini (prosecco and peach juice cocktail) in the bar, or lunch on the terrace.

Ca Pisani Hotel
(www.capisanihotel.it, Dorsoduro 979a, 041 240 1411), is a chic 4-star design property in my favorite Venice sestiere, that also offers guests cooking classes with Venetian native, Contessa Enrica Rocca. The class begins with shopping at the Rialto and then moves to the contessa's modern studio in the Dorsoduro.

The International Kitchen

(www.theinternationalkitchen.com) offers one day or longer cooking programs all over Italy—always with talented natives who share their life stories along with their recipes—making for a delicious and entertaining time. The Venice class is taught by Chef Patrizia, a charming, sprite-like *signora*, who teaches out of her palazzo apartment, near San Marco.

A Couple of Memorable Wine Bars near the Rialto:

Al Mercà, (Campo Cesare Battisti, San Polo 213)

All'Arco, (Calle Arco, San Polo 436)

Both of these are small, popular with locals, and serve inexpensive wines by the glass and delicious, classic Venetian snacks=*cichetti*.

Postcard From Naples: Snap Out Of It!

One of my favorite movie moments is in *Moonstruck* when Nicholas Cage tells Cher he loves her, she slaps him and barks, "Snap out of it!" It reminds me of the no holds-barred passion I grew up with. Like "Moonstruck", my childhood on the Jersey Shore was full of first generation immigrants from southern Italy--those folks who brought to America great things like pizza, sfogliatelle, and my personal favorite: high volume emotional outbursts.

It's behavior I never see in Los Angeles. Here, if a guy says "I love you" right after he meets you, the gal smiles sweetly and suggests medication. That's why it was so refreshing to go to the source of the noisy passion I was nursed on: Naples, Italy.

It was all so familiar from the moment I hit the street. There they were: look-alikes of those broad expressive faces and hands flying through the air that entertained me as a kid.

At the caffe, I order a cappuccino and BAM! Even before my milk is steamed, the show begins with shouts of "No, NO!" from the caffe owner. He waves his arms in protest against a pleading signor in a suit. *Signore* Suit simply wants to leave something behind the counter: a live wriggling eel. The eel, after all, is in a bag; he'd just bought it from the fish cart outside. Thick open palmed "No" hands debate pinched *"Per favore"* fingers. This is nothing like my quiet LA Starbucks, where hands only move to click laptops and cell phones.

And I definitely know I'm not in Los Angeles when I get to the park and there are no Mommies calmly offering their children choices: "Kyle you can either get in the car or have a time out." Here in the Piazza Communale exasperated Mammas yell, *"Aldo, vieni qua!"* Aldo keeps kicking his soccer ball until Mamma grabs him by the collar and drags the screaming kid to the bus.

Later, at the trattoria, our waiter, Marco bellows: *"Spaghetti, gnocchi!"* He's not angry, just passionate about pasta. This is no Beverly Hills lunch spot, where servers whisper specials like "Pan-seared Ahi Tuna over Papaya Coulis," as if it were a rare disease.

Outside, I join a crowd gathered for a puppet show starring Pucinella, the mascot of Naples. We watch that rascal clown declare his love for a wide-eyed signorina puppet. Pucinella goes in for a kiss, signorina grabs a baseball bat and whacks poor "Puch" mercilessly. It's the cartoon version of Cher's "Snap out of it" *Moonstruck* slap. As we all applaud, a teenager on a Vespa bursts through the crowd to speed down an alley. Every one of us startled grown-ups lift our arms: *"AY!"*

I catch my reflection in a bakery window. That's me: framed by *baba* and *sfogliatelle*, hands raised, mouth open, with all the other five foot tall, olive-skinned ladies. I've become a member of the chorus in the land of my ancestors. It feels *fantastico* to snap out of it.

***

Some Naples Advice:

Most this story takes place in Naples' **Quartieri Spagnoli**, (Spanish Quarter), one of my favorite neighborhoods on earth. I rented an apartment there once, and the fight about the eel took place in a caffe on Via Concezione a Montecalvario.

On weekday mornings, you'll find the **Pignasecca Market**, with buckets full of glistening fish, baskets overflowing with *friarielli* (those tasty bitter greens), and sellers bellowing in operatic voices. Stop by **Panificio Vincenzo Coppola** (Via Pignasecca 35) for *taralle*, studded with almonds.

Eat:

Trattoria Nennella (Vico Lungo Teatro Nuovo 103, closed Sun). This is where the waiter bellows the specials, and you'll always be served homey, delicious food. It's been run by the same family for over 60 years—plenty of laughs to be shared with this gang as you *mangia*.

Osteria Rosa dei Venti (Vico Lungo del Gelso 110) I had one of the best lasagnas of my life in this humble, family run spot.

Stay:

Maria Mari B&B www.bbmarianapoli.com, A cozy B&B, run by a kind and helpful couple, with sweetly decorated rooms, and windows overlooking a colorful alley.

Hotel Il Convento, www.hotelilconvento.com, a lovely, restored 17th century palace turned 3-star hotel, offering tranquility in this lively neighborhood.

Letter from Sicily:
Ingrid, Me, and Stromboli

I am climbing to the top of the island of Stromboli, to get an up close experience of one of the world's most famous volcanoes. I keep flashing back to Ingrid Bergman, in absolute glamorous distress, stumbling along this same route in the 1950 movie. She plays Karin, a Lithuanian World War II refugee, who marries an Italian POW. The husband turns out to be a tyrant who takes her to his homeland desolate island, where she's surrounded by mean village crones.

In the final scene of *Stromboli*, she desperately tries to get to Ginostra, on the other side, where she can catch a boat and escape. She's wearing a pretty print dress, choking as clouds of smoke and ash billow around her. When she reaches the top of Stromboli, she realizes it's impossible—the volcano explodes below her—there's no way around it. Ingrid/Karin cries out to the heavens: "My God, help me!" She collapses in agony and tears. The camera pulls in for a close-up of what must be the most beautiful crier who ever lived: those cheek bones, perfectly arched eyebrows, the full lips.

On my lips is the sweet taste of scrumptious banana and chocolate gelato I just ate in the piazza below. Ingrid is remembered in that piazza with a bar named in her honor. Close by is a rose stucco house with a plaque on it that says this is where she lived with Roberto Rossellini in the spring of 1949, when he directed her in this movie. They fell madly in love during the making of *Stromboli*, though they were both married to others. Americans and Italians reacted with shock and disapproval to the brazen scandal. In Hollywood, where Ingrid was beloved for her roles in *Casablanca* and *Joan of Arc*, her rep plummeted, (in her words), "from a saint to a whore."

I remember Ingrid in the movie now, with a hand on her belly, as she struggled up this path— she was pregnant with Roberto's child at the time. The filming experience was chaotic. She had come here because she was impressed with the realism of Rossellini's films—*Open City* and *Paesan*. They were such a contrast to the glitzy fantasy pics of Tinseltown in the 1940s. Ingrid wrote Roberto a letter, asking if he'd use her in a movie, and he obliged. But little did she know she'd wind up in such a backward spot.

These days, my Stromboli is full of happy tourists. The island is part of a group of eight, called the Aeolians, scattered in the Tyrrhenian Sea, between the toe of Italy's boot and the northeastern shore of Sicily. It's become a dreamy place for travelers, who take ferries from port to port, to luxuriate in thermal springs, swim in lovely coves, and eat delicious seafood. Stromboli is the most dramatic of the bunch. Every 15 to 20 minutes there's a rumble and explosion of fiery red rocks from its top.

Strombolians are not rattled in the least by the eruptions. They call their volcano, Iddu, ("He"), as though it's just their grumpy old Papa above them, periodically belching smoke and fire. There haven't been major eruptions recently, but still, for safety reasons, it's illegal to walk to the top on your own. Travelers like me and my fellow Country Walkers gang join Stromboli's hiking outfits, which start the climb in the late afternoon so we'll reach the top by sunset.

At the trail head, our handsome, bearded guide Mario gathers the 20 of us—a mix of Americans and Italians, and asks, "Who is the slowest?" Without missing a beat, a 60-something year old Brunhilda type *signora* steps up with her walking stick. "Our leader!," Mario announces. *La Signora* raises her arms in triumph, the evening's goddess.

What a genius start. I can't stand speedsters leading group hikes, making us happy wanderer types feel pathetic. We start off at a steady pace, up a switch-back path that takes us on a 3000 feet ascent. It begins narrow and rocky, surrounded by cactus, broom, and caper bushes. The salty smell of the sea fades the higher we go, there's less green and more rock. We're surrounded by views of the sun setting into the sparkling Tyrrhenian, dotted with bobbing fishing boats, and ferries gliding by. Seagulls swoop overhead. The air gets cooler. Mario stops us every thousand feet, about every hour, for a rest. Sweaty and thirsty, we guzzle refreshment from our water bottles.

Anticipation mounts. Stromboli has intrigued me ever since I first saw that movie. A few years ago, I stayed on the chic Aeolian Island of Panarea, and watched the volcano explode in the distance from a lounge chair on the terrace of

Hotel La Raya. On another trip, there was an after dinner boat ride that took us offshore to dock in the darkness, with the star-filled sky overhead. The boat cut its motor, and in silence we all faced the island. Then came a low rumble, a boom, and BAM! Fireworks lit up the night.

I hear that rumbling now as we finally reach the ridge. We all line up at the edge, looking into the smoky earth below, a sulfur smell tingles my nose. The show revs up, with CRACK—BOOM, a wave of heat rises, and then the red-gold explosion. There's applause, cheers, cameras flash.

One of the gang I've been hiking with all week is Odin, a lanky geologist, who crouches with his camera for shots, then leaps into the air, thrilled with the spectacle. He turns to another hiker, and I see his hands working, explaining about what's going on that's making this marvelous display. I stand with Bonnie, a family therapist, who's become my walking buddy during this week. We're enjoying imagining this is happening as the ancient Romans said it did. They believed the God Vulcan (he of anger management problems), lived underground. He was married to Aphrodite, that gad-about Goddess of Love and Beauty, and when she would leave him for affairs with others, he'd act out, lighting a fire in his cave to express his rage to the world.

Bonnie and I find a place to sit and unpack our Scaccia—oil soaked thin bread, stuffed with cheese, olives, sundried tomatoes, and greens. Heavenly.

We're right where Ingrid's character, Karin, collapsed in defeat, in *Stromboli*, the movie. As director Rossellini saw it, his final Stromboli scene symbolized the surrender of ego to God=the inescapable force of nature.

Karin came here to escape. We came to discover--a goofy looking bunch, wearing regulation helmets, bundled up in hiking clothes.

The sunset casts golden rays above us. Stromboli explodes once more and we gasp in awe over the wonder of it.

****

Stromboli Advice:

This climb was led by **Magmatrek** (www.magmatrek.it), multilingual pros who regularly lead groups to the top of Stromboli in the afternoons. You can also hire them as private guides, if you'd rather not go with the group. You'll need good hiking shoes, and dress in layers, as it gets chilly and windy at the top.

Country Walkers (www.countrywalkers.com) is an excellent company for group hikes all over Italy, and they also offer self-guided and private tours. Their guides are natives, everything is seamlessly planned so trips run leisurely, and you get an authentic immersion experience.

More Fun in Stromboli:

Ritrovo Ingrid (Piazza San Vincenzo), is dramatically set on a hilltop, with stunning views, and offers delicious granite (traditional Sicilian flavored ices) and gelato. If you face the piazza church, and take the path to the right of it, you'll find the red stucco villa with a plaque on it, commemorating the great love affair of Roberto Rossellini and Ingrid Bergman.

Eat:

Trattoria ai Gechi (Vico Salina, 338 357 7559), A cozy, welcoming place for delicious fresh seafood and classic Sicilian Pasta alla Norma (with eggplant, tomatoes, basil, and cheese).

Zurro (Localita Marina Via Picone 18, 090 986 283), The seaside setting is lovely, the chef is passionate and eccentric, offering a menu that changes daily. Seafood, including ravioli stuffed with fish and tomato, is spectacular. Save room for desserts, such as chocolate cake and tiramisu. Pricey, but worth it.

Stay:

Hotel Miramare (www.miramarestromboli.it, via Vito Nunziate 3, 090 986 047), a charming 3-star, set on the Ficogrande (black beach). Rooms have terraces, the breakfast buffet is abundant and fresh. The hotel also has a Dependance, **Casa Limone**, a 4-room B&B accommodation, 50-steps up the hill. *Thanks to Margaret Cowan, of Mamma Margaret & Friends Cooking Adventures in Italy (www.italycookingschools.com), for the tip about this place.*

Letter from Puglia:
A Link in the Chain

I spotted her watering geraniums in the whitewashed alley. To anyone else the 70-something year old with the loose grey bun, flowery smock and thick ankles stuffed into orthopedic shoes was just another woman in Polignano a Mare, a sleepy seaside town in southern Italy. But to me, the sight of this *signora* who so resembled my immigrant grandmother, seemed to whisper: "Welcome Home."

La Signora sensed me watching her, turned and gave me a *"Buon giorno."* I rushed to explain what I was doing lurking about her neighborhood—that I was from America, on a bike trip with a group. And then I slipped in,

"*Mia nonna e nata a Bari*" (My nana was born in Bari), the capital of the region.

The words had an *abracadabra* effect. *La Signora*'s eyes lit up, she launched into a sweet ramble, too fast for me to understand every word, circling her jiggly arms around my face, saying she could see my *Nonna* in my dark eyes. I nodded along, feeling a deep-in-the-bloodline connection. I could smell tomato sauce wafting out her beaded doorway, caught sight of steam rising from a spaghetti pot on her stove. Not wanting to keep her from lunch, I gave her an *arrivederci,* then headed for the ristorante where my biking group had planned to meet.

I'm not a big fan of group travel, but this was working out. I'd always wanted to do Italy by bike, and signed up with Backroads for Puglia, when I read it was "Italy's flattest region."

"*Mia nonna e nata e Bari*" was the extra pull. The story goes that my great-grandfather's job at the Italian post office transferred him from the family home in the region of Molise, to Puglia, in the heel of the boot. I imagined my great-grandmother, already the mother of four at the time, leaving her little mountain village, moving to Bari, a port town on the Adriatic, and giving birth to Nana, as we called her.

Was it a hardship or a treat to be by the sea? An inspiration for my Nana's love for the ocean that I shared with her when we would walk the boardwalk near her summer house on the Jersey shore?

The Backroads trip was expertly organized, so we had group dinners at night—me and six other couples--but on the day rides we were free to follow the route according to our own style. "It's your vacation," said Erin, the perky tour guide, on the first night we gathered for cocktails to get the lowdown of the week.

So there was Patsy, who'd get in the *Backroads* van after the morning ride and go back to our luxury accommodations to relax by the pool. On the other end of the spectrum, senior citizen hot-doggers Laurie and Bob would be the first ones out in the morning, loading up on snacks from the van, speeding away, skipping lunch and taking the most challenging afternoon routes for uphill workouts. My approach was lagging behind to take pictures or poking around the small town lunch destinations, getting distracted by nana look-alikes.

The hilltop village of Locorotondo turned out to be the mother lode for my quest. Weaving through the circular maze of white stone buildings that make up the historic center, at every corner an appropriate character appeared: A woman in a long brown dress at a brass spigot filling up a water bottle, another seated under an arbor of violet bougainvillea crocheting a doily. The winner was the plump signora on a balcony hanging laundry. When she spotted me with my camera, she took off her apron and rushed down to strike a pose in front of a Roman archway. This time *"Mia nonna e nata a Bari"* brought me a crushing embrace followed by a scramble for a pen, as she wrote down her address and asked me to send her the photo.

What did Puglia look like to my relatives a hundred years ago? I could never imagine my Nana or any of her sisters getting near to straddling a bike seat—it was a huge deal for them to even sit on those curvy painted benches when they'd join me on the Merry Go Round. I'd never seen any of them in anything but dresses, and none of them even drove cars. But maybe as children they rode in a horse-drawn carriage through these farm roads I pedaled. Maybe those past generations marveled at the same sights I did--hills of vineyards, cherry trees heavy with deep red clusters of fruit, fields of crimson poppies and golden zucchini flowers. And most gasp-inspiring:

endless fields of olive trees--the oldest in Italy, with humongous trunks, the size of Volkswagens.

It was the end of pruning season--the smell of burning olive tree branches mixed with blooming jasmine was sublime. Farmers along the way gave us friendly waves and beeps, unaccustomed to seeing strangers in their quiet terrain.

Quiet that is, except for my groans as I pedaled up one of the few challenging hills. I cursed myself for not joining Patsy in the van, regretted not working out harder pre-trip. Yikes, I was feeling old.

My mind that had been filled with cozy Nana thoughts inspired by the *signoras* I'd seen, began to turn dark. Spooky memories of Nana's final decade, after my grandfather died, started to seep in, as sweat dripped down my back. Nana's transformation was a horror--from soft bosomy matriarch standing at the stove with the wooden spoon, to a pale skeleton lying in bed, glassy-eyed, dentureless, whimpering, "I want to die…why won't he take me?"

My 20-something year old self had zero compassion for this lamenting invalid who turned my mother into a nervous, angry wreck. I'd do my part when I'd visit home in the summers, sitting bedside, watching the clock flip through slow moving minutes. Then I'd pat Nana's wrinkled hand she kept clutched around a rosary, and finally walk out of that room, drenched in guilt.

When the inevitable phone call came to my San Francisco apartment late one night, my father flatly broke the news. With my mother and aunt sitting beside her in the suffering room, Nana had slipped away, calling out, forever mysteriously, "Daddy, hurry…"

My body was tightening pushing up the hill, my throat hardened. I was just about to quit and walk it, when I realized I'd reached the top. Panting, heart racing, I stopped to take it in: a green valley stretched out before me. And for the first time I saw those architectural treasures Puglia is famous for: *trulli*-small white cone-shaped houses from the Middle Ages. I blinked at the lovely vision. The lump in my throat dissolved. Down came the tears—awe on top of pain on top of regrets mixed with a rise of compassion that was coming on, it seemed to me, decades too late.

"Woo-hoo, you Go Girl!"

It was tour guide Erin, who had been bringing up the rear…in this case, me. I high-fived her as best as my trembling hand could, and not wanting her to see my emotionally devastated state, began the downward ride.

There was nowhere to go from here but down to paradise, let go of the brakes and allow nature--the inevitable rush of euphoria to take over.

A comforting thought crept in: *Choose your version.* And as happens more often than not in Italy, a deep peace washed through me, sweet memories returned.

I slowed down as I hit the flat coast road, took it through the village of Savelletri, and sure enough caught sight of a *signora* in a housecoat washing her steps. Opposite her stood a statue of the Blessed Virgin, pure white against the blue Adriatic and sky. As it was May, the month of Mary, a wreath of flowers lay at her feet to honor her.

I said a silent *Ave Maria*, grateful for the maternal line that pulls me back to Italy again and again. And feeling strengthened by the days of cycling, the wind at my back, and most of all the connection to my ancestral home, I picked up speed, bordered by the sparkling sea on one side, and on the other, those old gnarled olive trees, bursting with buds of spring.   .

Puglia Advice:

This story is from a trip I took with Backroads, www.backroads.com. I loved the experience so much I've gone back with them to ride around Sicily. They take you on ingenious routes, choose primo accommodations and authentic restaurants, and balance itineraries out for every level.

La Taverna del Duca (Via Papatotero 3, 080 431 3007, Locorotondo), in that hilltop village that was the mother lode for nana-look-alikes, was where I had one of the most memorable meals of the trip: a simple dish of orechiette (Puglia's signature tiny ear-shaped pasta) and tomato sauce. The Taverna is a small, humble spot, with a blackboard menu that changes daily.

Pizzeria di Cosimo, (Via Giovanni Modugno 31, 080 504 1513, **Bari**), is a great place in the capital city to elbow in with the locals for pizza and *panzerotti*=typical Pugliese fried turnovers stuffed with cheese and tomatoes.

Conversano, is a beautifully restored Medieval village, southeast of Bari—a great base to explore the whole Valle d'Itria, where vineyards, olive groves, and trulli enchant. Village highlights are an impressive Norman Castle and Romanesque Cathedral.

In Conversano,

Eat at Pasha (www.pashaconversano.it, Piazza Castello 5/7, 080 495 1079), the fanciest restaurant in the village, where Mamma Maria cooks delicious, upscale renditions of Pugliese classics, and her son Antonello oversees the elegant dining room.

Stay at Corte Altavilla Relais & Charme (www.cortealtavilla.it, Via Goffredo Altavilla 8, 080 495 9668). Every room is unique in this 4-star, a masterfully restored former castle, smack in the middle of the historic center. Modern comforts blend with history here, and the hotel has a fabulous spa and rooftop restaurant.

Agriturismo Montepaolo (www.montepaolo.it, 080 495 5087), on the outskirts of **Conversano**, is also a great place to stay—a renovated 16th century farm estate, featuring lovely accommodations, decorated with owner Niny Bassi's handpainted furniture. Niny is also an excellent chef, serving cucina povera in style—reserve for a memorable lunch, even if you're not staying there.

Letter from Umbria: The Truffle Hunt

Once upon a time I stood in a grand piazza, waiting for a stranger to arrive and take me into a forest for a truffle hunt. It was dark. I was shivering. And all alone.

What the hell was I doing here at 6:25 in the a.m.?

Here, being Gubbio, a medieval village in the region of Umbria. It's a fairytale of a place: all done up in ivory stone--towers, Romanesque churches, palazzos-tucked into a hillside, surrounded by a shimmering green forest.

I was drawn to Gubbio by the treasures that grow in that forest: Truffles. Warty, misshapen, delicious tubers. Sacred mysteries of the gourmet world. They can't be cultivated, but grow amidst the roots of trees. In Italy they're dug up by trained dogs, rather than pigs that the French use, as Italians discovered that dogs are less likely to gobble up what they sniff out.

Black truffles are found in Gubbio June through April. November through January is the season for pricey white truffles. The smell of these goodies is a knock-out: earthy, musky, with a garlicky, peppery hint—what Romans called "vaguely sexual." The Catholic Church caught on to their seductive nature in the Middle Ages and banned truffles, declaring that they surely came straight from the devil.

My first whiff of truffles came on an autumn visit to Pisa. I entered a trattoria, and the whole room reeked of an enticing, deep aroma. I immediately checked out what the locals were eating, and ordered *tartufi* shaved over *bistecca*. One bite and I was hooked. Later, in a Los Angeles cooking class, the teacher/chef passed around a white truffle he'd paid $2500 for at an auction, and teased that he'd be charging us students ten dollars a sniff.

All week in Gubbio I've been devilishly indulging in truffles—sprinkled over tagliatelle, eggs, pork loin. Stuffed into a rabbit, in cheese. Every morning I slather truffle butter over my breakfast bread. When Paolo, the hotel concierge, offered to find me a truffle hunter I could tag along with, I jumped at the chance. It's not like anybody can randomly tap a hunter on a shoulder and say, "Take me with you." This is serious-big-bucks-making-biz, and hunters are secretive about their methods and spots.

"I know a guy," Paolo whispered. "Marino Aringolo is the best *trifolau* (truffle hunter) in all of Gubbio."

I'd gotten to like Paolo over my Gubbio days--a Poindexter-ish, 30-something fellow--forever pumped to show off his village to a *giornalista Americana*. Unlike more popular Umbrian spots (such as Perugia and Assisi), Gubbio has stayed under the tourist radar. But following Paolo I discovered it's got major claims to fame.

First of all, I'm staying at a Palazzo, (now the Hotel Relais Ducale), that once was the home of the Duke of Montefeltro. That means nothing until Paolo shows me the famous Piero della Francesca portrait of a Renaissance man in profile wearing a red cap, with a huge schnozola and tells me: "The Duke had to be painted in profile, because the whole other side of his face was destroyed in a joust. He had a great time here in Gubbio."

As I follow Paolo up and down the cobblestoned *vias*, he's got stories at every turn: "Here's the San Francesco church, that was once the home of the Spadalonga family--they were wool makers. In the 12th century, when a guy named Francis walked to Gubbio from Assisi, (NAKED—after he'd taken his vow of poverty), the Spadalongas threw a grey wool cloak over him. That became the first vestment of the Franciscan friars. Saint Francis stuck around and miraculously tamed a wolf in the forest who had been terrorizing the whole village. And here's the Roman theatre, built under the order of Juluis Caesar, who came through Gubbio on his campaign against Pompey, after saying those famous words, "The Die is Cast." And this is the Fountain of the Mad. Run around it three times, splash yourself, and you can officially be declared insane." No kidding about that last one--shops surrounding the fountain sell certificates that can get you into an asylum.

Paolo also wasn't kidding when he dropped the gulp-inspiring: "Marino the Truffle Hunter will pick you up in the piazza tomorrow…at 6:30 a.m."

The thought of actually dealing with another human being pre-caffe was daunting. Still, this timing meant Marino was the real deal. Early-early morn is *primo* for truffle hunting—when the chill intensifies the smell of the tubers so dogs can more easily sniff them out, and darkness keeps the hunter's moves secret. These days, in more well known truffle places, such as Alba, in the northern region of Piedmont, a cottage industry of hunting tours has been built up. Many are fakes, stocked with pre-planted truffles, so customers will come away satisfied.

Good man Paolo set me up with authentic. Authentic is often not pretty. Now, at 6:30 on the dot, dim yellow headlights appear and a dusty gray hatchback inches towards me. I can barely make out the driver who rolls down his window and says in a soft, low voice: *"Susanna?"*

I see two caged dogs in the back of the car—a black and a tan, and a rusty, dangerous looking gardening hoe. And then I'm face-to-face with Marino. Not a trace of the Big Bad Wolf about him. He's a compact fellow--bald, with wire spectacles framing brown puppy dog eyes. The kind of guy who could walk into an LA casting office and get typed as "trusty handyman." Plus he pulls out a thermos of coffee and a cup for me. Bless him.

All's well until he takes a look at my feet. I'm wearing one of my favorite Italy purchases: suede-black-lace-up-to-the-shin-rubber-flat-soled boots that I scored in Rome years ago. They've been praised by many a galfriend, but clearly their appeal doesn't register with Marino. He rummages in the trunk and pulls out a pair of dirty rubber green high boots. "These will be better," he tells me. I can see immediately that they're at least three sizes too big, but Marino keeps making motions and encouraging sounds: "Try..."

It's a way-warped version of Prince Charming with the Glass Slipper. Back and forth we go, the middle-aged country guy and the stubborn city *signora*, all very civil, until the dogs in the cages start getting restless. Marino shrugs, gives up, and *Andiamo...*

I have a harder time shrugging. Figures I'd have shoe issues in Italy—the country worships footwear as much as pasta. But I couldn't have put on those boots-not just because they were so ugly, but they're so big I'd be tripping over myself...I think. Yes, I've been in situations before with close galfriends where I've been told "re-think the shoes." They always end with a laugh and a switch. But this Marino shoe thing sets me in another direction. I fear I've wrecked a trifolau's morning.

Now he's regretting saying yes to Paolo and has to put up with an improperly shod tag-a-long to his all important truffle hunting job. I'm like the dud-of-a-girl at the pool party who forgets her bathing suit and tries to act like it's no big deal when she dives in wearing her bra and panties.

As we wind away from *il centro storico*, I try to make up for getting off on the wrong foot (no pun intended), by praising Marino's hometown.

He counters with the classic Italian interview: "Where's your husband?"

"At home in Los Angeles, working…" And I imagine him in a freeway traffic jam, as our road turns to gravel, then dirt.

Marino tells me he's the father of three grown girls, and has a grandson. I see the laugh crinkles around his eyes and imagine him bouncing that baby boy on his knee.

We stop at the edge of the forest. "We look here for *tartufi bianchi*," Marino says. Even though it's October, a couple of weeks early, maybe we'll get lucky and find a high-priced treasure.

Out of the cages pop the dogs--a black lab he calls "Fee-doh" and "Lah-dee," a tan pointer, eager for foraging. Clearly they're the hunter's best friends—Marino pats them and they bound ahead to the darkness.

I'm the babe in the woods here--Marino leading the way with his flashlight...not a gingerbread hut or gnome in sight. He's been hunting in these woods for 40 years, and knows every step of the way. There are no paths. The dogs are the smartest among us—their sense of smell is a thousand times stronger than ours. The forest floor is damp and soft with fallen leaves. The only sound is our footsteps and the rustling of Fido and Lady through ferns and shrubs.

"*Fa piano, guarda bene,*" (Go slow, look well), Marino calls out to them, in the kindest of dog-loving voices.

Suddenly they stop to paw intently at a mound of dirt at the base of an oak. Marino rushes over, shoos them away, kneels down, and starts digging. I join him as he smells the dirt. To me, it smells, *truffle-ish.*

I'm sniffing away with Marino, getting keyed up that we just may uncover a white truffle. Maybe I'll be Marino's good luck charm, which would surely make up for our shoe issue. But digging only leads to more *truffle-ish* smelling dirt.

We go on, criss-crossing a creek, where he points out all the spots where his dogs dug up *tartufi bianchi* in past years. *"Così,"* he says, holding his hands in the shape of a porridge bowl, to show how big those truffles were.

I know he's disappointed, but I don't know how to say to him that it's so amazing just being in this forest, I don't care if we find truffles or not. My boots are soggy and covered in mud. I've lost track of time, caught up in this foraging dance Marino's taking me through as we follow the creek, the dogs rustling about as our chorus. Marino's a gracious leader—at turns reaching out with his hand, elbow, forearm to help me climb up the steep spots or steady my jumps across logs. He holds back shrub branches as valiantly as a prince opening a carriage door.

And then we come to a spot where the creek is so wide there's no way to leap across it. Marino looks at my feet, gives a little sigh. The water is too deep for me to slush through. Now I have to admit it: Wrong Shoes. He should just leave idiot me here in the mud. This is the point in the Hansel and Gretel version where big white ducks appear and we go across on their backs. But no ducks in sight. Instead Marino asks:

"*Sulle spalle o cosi bambina?*"==On my shoulders or like a baby?

My first response is the logical: "I'm too fat."

To which he kindly replies: "50 kilos?"

There's no fighting with this. I choose *bambina*. He holds out his arms and I slip in.

The carry is only a few seconds, but it wooshes me way back to my 5-year old self— faking sleep on the living room couch so my father would have to pick me up, carry me to bed, and tuck me in. Surrender. Bliss.

We wind up out of the dark forest, into a sunlit, warm meadow. "*Tartufi neri*==black truffles," Marino says.

Fido and Lady rush to the meadow's border of trees, furiously paw and… *ta-da*—they've found them. They rise up with black truffles in their jaws that Marino swiftly grabs. He opens up his vest pocket, takes out a baggie full of mortadella chunks and tosses them out as rewards. Last night they weren't fed dinner in preparation for this hunt, so they'd be primed to dig up anything edible. They chomp, their tails wag. Then recharged, they bound back to the trees for another round of sniff and dig.

Within 15 minutes they've dug up enough black truffles to practically fill my baseball cap. Some small as pebbles, others big as cauliflowers. It's as if we've switched movie sets, from a surreal film in that forest to an action packed lightning speed romp up here. I'm knocked out, inhaling what the folks around here call "black diamonds."

Marino takes a seat on the grass, and pulls a Merit cigarette out of his vest pocket. The work is done, he'll be helping one of his daughters move this afternoon, he says. Fido and Lady romp around us, and as we head back to the car, Marino pats and congratulates them for a job well done. In the bright sunlight I look down and see from the knees down I'm covered in mud, a piglet.

When Marino drops me off at the Piazza Grande, he insists I keep the truffles. "Share them with your friends in Rome," he tells me. The church bells clang as I watch him drive away.

Was that a dream? I'm thinking, as I shave my truffles over *taglietelle* in my friends' kitchen in Rome the next night. They toast me for bringing back such delicious booty.

I swirl the pasta around my fork, thinking of my mother's "Never get in a car with a stranger" warning. And the whole familiar Mommy Medley: The Car and The Stranger, The Car Accident and

The Clean Underwear, The Good Job and The Pension—all of which I've so long ignored. Somehow I turned out trusting, known to ask strangers at caffes to watch my laptop when I have to get up to go pee, or take a dive into the ocean with my purse left on a beach chair.

In Italy, I show up, and no matter what shoes I'm wearing, I'm somehow blessed with surprises of kindness in abundance. Such as a Prince Charming, in the form of a saintly forager, who gave me black diamonds.

The *tagliatelle al tartufo* is delicious. And we gratefully all live happily ever after.

****

Gubbio Advice:

Hotel Relais Ducale (www.relaisducale.com, Via Galeotti 19, 075 922 0157), right on the Piazza Grande, immerses you into the elegant history of Gubbio. Tastefully decorated rooms offer stunning views of the town and surrounding forest, the staff is enthusiastic and generously accommodating at every turn.

Eat:

Taverna del Lupo (www.tavernadellupo.it, Via Ansidei 21, 075 9274368, Closed Monday). Legend says this is the spot where Saint Francis tamed the terrorizing lupo=wolf of Gubbio. The elegant restaurant serves up excellent Umbrian fare, with many dishes featuring truffles, along with a distinctive wine selection.

Osteria dei Re (www.osteriadeire.com, Via Cavour 15, 075 9222504, Closed Wednesday), A folksy place where local wine is served in tumblers, along with platters of cured meats and delicious pastas.

Tuesday is Market Day, and you'll enjoy the lively scene that covers the Piazza 40 Martiri in the lower part of town.

Gubbio is also home to colorful yearly events:

Race of the Candles (Corsa dei Ceri, www.ceri.it, May 15). This festival harkens back to medieval days, honoring the town's Saint Ubaldo. The main event, surrounded by music and pageantry, features townspeople racing up the hill, holding three large wooden statues. Reservations for hotels during this time must be made well in advance.

Cross Bow Tournament (Palio della Balestra, www.balestrierigubbio.com, Last Sunday in May). The Piazza Grande is the scene of this contest between cross bow shooters from Gubbio and Sansepolcro, accompanied by impressive shows by Gubbio's Sbandieratori=Flag Throwers.

Truffle Festival (Tartufo in Tavola, www.tartufointavola.it, late October) The whole town celebrates the white truffle with tastings and music filling Gubbio's piazzas and restaurants.

The World's Biggest Christmas Tree (Albero di Natale, www.alberodigubbio.com, December 7-January 10), The year ends with colorful lights arranged in a Christmas tree shape on Monte Ingino, the natural background that rises above Gubbio. Thousands come to admire the spectacle, which shines over the town all through the holiday season.

About the Author

Italian American Susan Van Allen has written about Italian travel for National Public Radio, magazines, newspapers, and websites. She is the author of *100 Places in Italy Every Woman Should Go*, and the *Golden Days in Italy* blog. When she's not traveling to Italy, she lives in Los Angeles with her husband and makes scrumptious lasagnas.

More info: www.susanvanallen.com.

Made in the USA
Middletown, DE
28 May 2015